A GUIDE TO
HISTORIC GLENDIVE

This book was made possible in part by funding
from the Montana Cultural Trust, the Frontier Gateway
Museum, and the Yellowstone Caviar Grant Fund.

Montana Mainstreets

VOLUME TWO

A GUIDE TO

HISTORIC GLENDIVE

WITH A PREFACE BY
Paul Putz, State Historic Preservation Officer of Montana

AND AN AFTERWORD BY
Louise Cross, Curator of the Frontier Gateway
Museum, Glendive

MONTANA
HISTORICAL
SOCIETY
PRESS

COVER IMAGE Wool wagons in Glendive, Montana, no date, MHS Photo Archives
COVER DESIGN Kathryn Fehlig
BOOK DESIGN Arrow Graphics, Missoula
TYPESET IN Stempel Schneidler

All of the images reproduced in this book came from either Frontier Gateway Museum, Glendive (FGM); Montana Historical Society Library (MHS Library); Montana Historical Society Photograph Archives (MHS Photo Archives); or State Historic Preservation Office, Helena (SHPO), and are credited in the captions.

PRINTED BY Advanced Litho Printing, Great Falls

MONTANA
CULTURAL
TRUST

Partial funding for this project was provided by Montana's Cultural Trust.

98 99 00 01 02 03 04 05 06   10 9 8 7 6 5 4 3 2 1

ISBN 0-917298-58-6

LIBRARY OF CONGRESS CATALOGING-IN-PUBLICATION DATA

Guide to historic Glendive / with a preface by Paul Putz ; and an afterword by Louise Cross.
    p.   cm. — (Montana mainstreets ; v. 2)
    Includes bibliographical references and index.
    ISBN 0-917298-58-6 (alk. paper)
    1. Glendive (Mont.)—Tours. 2. Historic sites—Montana—Glendive—Guidebooks. 3. Glendive (Mont.)—History. I. Montana Historical Society. II. Series.
F739.G55G85   1998
978.6'24—dc21   98-37699
                                                                    CIP

Contents

Acknowledgments

THIS BOOK is the product of many people's labor. Bill Babcock wrote the original State Historic Preservation Office survey of Glendive; Marge Jacobson typed an early draft of the manuscript; Ellen Baumler, coordinator of the National Register sign program, reviewed the text and provided additional research; and Ken Sievert created the line art. Phi Alpha Theta interns Chris Nelson and Randi Webb, designers Kathryn Fehlig and Kitty Herrin, and mapmaker Bill Vaughn all also materially aided the completion of *Guide to Historic Glendive*. In addition to writing the preface, State Historic Preservation Officer Paul Putz offered his support for the original grant for the Mainstreet series, which helped to secure much needed and appreciated funding from the Montana Cultural Trust.

This book would not have been possible without the hard work of a committee of interested Glendive residents: Louise Cross, Curator of the Frontier Gateway Museum; Avis Anderson and Eileen Melby, authors of *Ranchers, Railroaders, and Retailers of Glendive*; and Linda Koncilya, director of the Glendive Chamber of Commerce. They reviewed the text, tracked down photographs, and aided the project in innumerable other ways. A special thank you is due to Louise Cross, who submitted the grant to the Yellowstone Caviar Fund and wrote the afterword; and to Avis Anderson, who coordinated the review process. Frontier Gateway Museum volunteer Audrey Avilla stepped in at the last moment to locate a final, critical photograph. Thanks also to former Glendive chamber director John Trangmoe, who responded to the Montana Historical Society Press's initial inquiries with enthusiasm and encouragement.

Preface

THIS BOOK, one in a series of guidebooks to historic communities in Montana, derives much of its information from research and inventories conducted through the State Historic Preservation Office to find properties eligible for listing on the National Register of Historic Places. The Register lists places important to national, state, and local history and recognizes neighborhoods, commercial areas, individual sites, and even landscapes to call attention to the role they played in the history of our nation.

The National Register's founders understood that local history was the foundation of our nation's heritage and that a National Register of Historic Places would be incomplete without locally significant sites. The criteria for registration span a broad range of possibilities: the Register includes sites associated with important people; those of unique, masterful, or representative construction; and those that illuminate broad historical patterns. Significant, too, are those places such as archaeological sites containing information contributing to our understanding of history and prehistory. Within this range it is possible to construct the story of the United States, the rich interrelationship of its peoples, the incredible dynamism of its inhabitants through the ages, and the expression of its revolutionary ideals.

Your tour of this community will be a tour of the past, an examination of how the town grew, who built it, what economic factors sustained it, and how the community evolved socially. It will be a tour of history in a local context. Of course, the history of our nation continues to unfold, but usually only places older than fifty years are eligible for listing on the National Register. For that reason, you will not find our more recent history in the annals of the Register or much of it between these pages. Nor, in this guide, will you find mention of every building or incident significant to this community. Much research remains to be done on our Montana towns. Many historic sites and neighborhoods that deserve recognition remain to be researched and recorded in the Register.

This book will introduce you to certain noteworthy sites. But because there is much more in this community worthy of investigation than this volume can cover, this guidebook series is also designed to help you learn how to read for yourself the history written on a town's streets in brick, board, and stone. Within this volume are descriptions of many visible, expressive, and delightful sites and an abundance of compelling stories. May they launch you into a continuing exploration of the history that surrounds us all.

PAUL PUTZ
State Historic Preservation
Officer of Montana

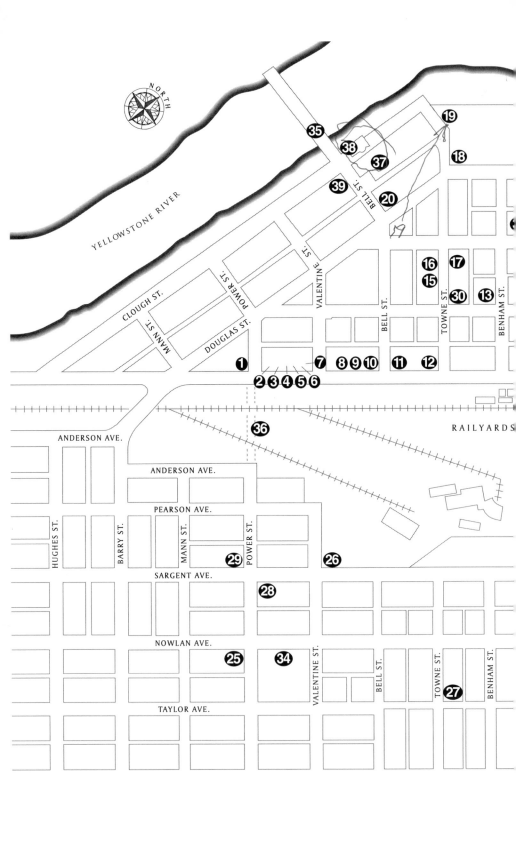

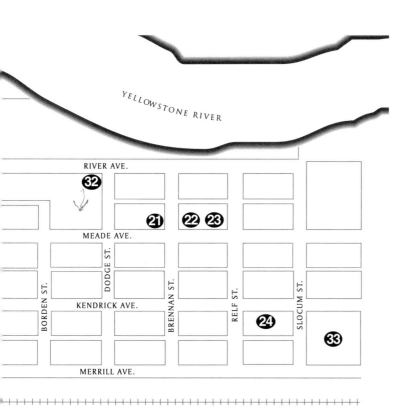

YELLOWSTONE RIVER

RIVER AVE.

32

MEADE AVE.

21　**22**　**23**

DODGE ST.

BORDEN ST.

KENDRICK AVE.

BRENNAN ST.

RELF ST.

SLOCUM ST.

24

33

MERRILL AVE.

GLENDIVE
HISTORIC SITES

BORDEN ST.

How to Use This Guide

Glendive started in anticipation of railroad.

GLENDIVE was a product of the Northern Pacific Railroad. During the nineteenth century, settlements sprang up overnight all along the routes forged across the country by the mighty steam engines, linking some of the most remote outposts of the nation in a way never before imagined. In Montana, especially, the railroad brought the outside world into the wild recesses of the frontier. The laying of tracks brought opportunity and a new worldview that was broader and more cosmopolitan than previously imaginable. Railroad towns like Glendive are a significant part of the legacy of this new industry.

In Montana as well as elsewhere the railroad changed the look of towns and cities along its route. Before the tracks swept across the vast Montana plains, goods that could not be manufactured locally had to be shipped overland from Salt Lake City or up the Missouri River to Fort Benton and then overland by mule team or heavy ox-drawn freight wagon via primitive roads and trade trails. The railroad offered unlimited shipping possibilities, and architecture and building in particular benefited from this new mode of transportation.

Prefabricated pieces of buildings, such as decorative stone, brick, metal storefronts, and large pieces of glass for display windows could be sent easily wherever the tracks led. This is clearly evident in Glendive with its widespread use of brick "imported" from Hebron, North Dakota, and other decorative stonework, cast metal embellishments, and glass storefronts that could not be manufactured locally.

The object of this guidebook is to help visitors learn to read Glendive's history in its architecture, to recognize the visual evidence of what is old and what is new, and to understand and appreciate the stages in between. This book does not tell the whole story of Glendive, nor does it take the visitor on a site-by-site walking tour of the town. It is designed, however, as a key to introduce some of Glendive's founders and historical and architectural patterns.

The first section of this book offers an overview of the town's history through World War II, with particular attention to the events that shaped Glendive's built environment. The next three sections are site specific and direct the reader's attention to Glendive's commercial, residential, and industrial streetscapes. The conclusion brings the present town into perspective and, finally, a bibliography is provided for those who wish to further their knowledge of this historic railroad town in the heart of Montana's ranching country. Enjoy your journey!

The 200 block of North Merrill Avenue about 1881 looking north. The building with the second-floor balcony is the Yellowstone Hotel. The civilized facade of the Hotel Harpster has fashionable brackets and narrow arched windows, characteristics of the Italianate style of architecture popular in the 1880s. Hitching posts are conveniently placed in front of the saloon. Courtesy FGM

Electricity in 1881 ?

The Gate City

THE TENACIOUS TOWN of Glendive, according to author Marian T. Place, was born "astraddle the tracks with its back to the river and its face toward the soaring badlands." It is a fitting portrayal of this lively community, rooted in railroad and ranching industries, which lies in the lower Yellowstone Valley about thirty miles from the North Dakota border and eighty-five miles above the confluence of the Yellowstone and Missouri rivers. As the entrance to the Yellowstone Valley, Glendive was nicknamed the "Gate City." Here the meandering Yellowstone River cuts through an area once thickly blanketed with native grasses. For generations this well-watered, prime grazing land sustained vast herds of buffalo and brought success to early ranchers.

J. R. Widmeyer, editor of the Glendive *Independent,* in 1896 described Glendive's setting as a "natural amphitheater, surrounded on almost every side by picturesquely rugged hills." The editor carefully avoided the term coined by French trappers, "mauvais terres pour traverser," meaning "lands difficult to travel," shortened to "mauvais terres," literally "bad lands." Town boosters viewed this nickname as a deterrent to settlement and, while an 1882 prospectus self-consciously explained that the corrugated arroyos made overland travel difficult, it stressed the small proportion of these curious features. Others less concerned with population growth described the veins of coal and colorful layers of sediment and red scoria as "Hell cooked over," fueling further unfavorable connotations. Visitors can view this natural kaleidoscope, the result of millions of years of wind and water erosion, at nearby Makoshika State Park.

Archaeological evidence near Glendive reveals human habitation 11,500 years ago at the Hagan site, discovered in a plowed field on the private property of rancher and early Glendive mayor Thomas F. Hagan. This National Historic Landmark was once an ancient village of earthen lodges where early farmers cultivated tobacco and squash; it may have been the home of the ancestors of Montana's Crow Indians. Later, Blackfeet, Crow, Assiniboine, and Sioux hunted the valley. Famous explorers and trappers like Sieur de la Verendrye and François Larocque passed through the area. William Clark camped near the mouth of Glendive Creek on August 1, 1806, as the Lewis and Clark Expedition returned from the Pacific.

Travelers such as John James Audubon and Father Pierre John DeSmet noted the region's abundant game and the unique geological formation of the badlands. One theory as to how the town got its name stems from this early period. Legend and local opinion have it that Sir George Gore, an Irish nobleman who undertook an ambitious and expensive three-year hunting trip to the American West in the 1850s, named Glendale Creek, which became Glendive on later maps. Sir George, the consummate "slob hunter," bagged some two thousand deer, elk, and buffalo on his trek through Montana; he had no use for sixteen hundred of them.

Military expeditions led by Captain William F. Raynolds, Lieutenant H. A. Maynadier, and Lieutenant John Mullan explored the area in the 1860s and reported its potential as stock and farm land. Maynadier speculated on steamboat traffic on the Yellowstone, but reported "much would have to be done before boats could run with profit." The United States Government recognized the area as Sioux land in the Harney-Sanborn Treaty of 1865. The 1868 Treaty of Fort Laramie again defined the land south of the Yellowstone as Sioux territory, but foreshadowed the later arrival of the Northern Pacific Railroad by providing for a right-of-way through the region.

Surveying for a northern transcontinental railroad route began in the late 1860s and determined that a townsite would eventually be located near Glendive Creek. The confluence of the Yellowstone River and Glendive Creek was strategically important as the first point west of Mandan, North Dakota, where steamboats could deliver construction supplies to railroad crews. Miners, ranchers, and the coming railroad encroached upon tribal hunting grounds and led to difficulties with native peoples. This prompted the United States Army to establish a series of small military posts in the region. General George Forsyth established Camp Canby, a fort and supply depot at Glendive Creek in 1873, just east of the future townsite, anticipating that the railroad would cross the Yellowstone River at that point. A few timbers found by archaeologists give evidence of the camp's close proximity to Glendive.

Railroad construction that began at St. Paul, Minnesota, in 1870 stalled at Bismarck, North Dakota, with the financial panic of 1873; rail crews resumed work in 1879. In the meantime, extermination of the buffalo on the Northern Plains eliminated the major sustenance of the Plains Indians and opened the vast grasslands to stock raising. The shipping of buffalo hides and bones was Glendive's first significant industry.

Midway between Bismarck and Billings, Glendive was an ideal place for the Northern Pacific's Yellowstone Division headquarters. A deep river channel close to the riverbank made the site an excellent steamboat landing as well. Because the railroad reached the Yellowstone River at Glendive, early planners envisioned complementing rail transportation with steamboats for easier access to Forts Buford and Benton.

By the end of 1880, tracks of the Northern Pacific were twenty-eight miles away from the small settlement, and the army cantonment became a boomtown where plenty of saloons and dance halls catered to railroad crews. A second theory about Glendive's name has to do with these rough beginnings. A man named Bob Glenn ran a well-known thirst emporium below the townsite that was colloquially known as "Glenn's dive": railroad men shortened the name of the settlement to Glendive.

As the tracks fast approached, officials decided not to route the line to the west bank of the Yellowstone River. The townsite relocated to the east side of the river where Glendive is today. The first residents hastily built tents and log huts to await the arrival of the first train. It finally lumbered into the townsite on July 5, 1881, adding steam from its engine to the sweltering 110-degree weather. When the first load of lumber arrived soon after, a building boom began, and by November Glendive had 150 houses.

The building boom that followed in the steam of the first locomotives replaced the temporary tents and mud-roofed log cabins, according to the Glendive *Times*, with "sightly structures, large business houses, stores and dwellings." By November 1881, businesses included four mercantiles, two hotels, four restaurants, a dry goods store, two blacksmiths, two butchers, and a livery stable. The town even boasted several physicians, a lawyer, a shoemaker, and a watchmaker. Building continued in the spring of 1882 when the last tent disappeared and the commercial district along Merrill Avenue emerged.

Merrill Avenue about 1883 looking north. Until about 1886, Glendive's first commercial buildings were wood frame. Many had false fronts, a common feature on the western frontier, which made buildings appear larger and more impressive. Courtesy FGM

By the end of February 1882, railroad-related buildings began to appear that shaped the town's character. The railroad by this time had laid more than five miles of sidetrack and constructed mammoth warehouses, a twelve-thousand-dollar waterworks, a freight depot, and the largest turntable on the line. Plans were ready for a roundhouse, a machine shop, and a blacksmith shop—all to be built of local brick. Henry Douglas, a former Northern Pacific commissary agent, built a local brickyard in the winter of 1881–82 for railroad-related buildings. The passenger depot and stockyards were completed soon after. However, none of these early buildings survives today.

Lumber for commercial and residential building had to be shipped from the east until the completed railroad line allowed shipping of pine and other construction lumber from the forests of Oregon and Washington. The scarcity of building materials hampered development as did the fact that the first bricks were earmarked for the railroad, delaying masonry construction of commercial buildings until 1886.

The railroad yards permanently divided Glendive into two halves. The terminal facilities, including the sidetracks, divided the town lengthwise while the spur line to the river marked the south edge of town. Sandwiched between railroad-related buildings and the steamboat landing, the west side along Merrill Avenue became the logical commercial center. Industrial buildings and utilities located close to the river, near the spur line.

Geography determined the layout of Glendive, confined between the Yellowstone River to the west and the bluffs to the east. Railroad officials believed that the location on Sage Brush Flats was wide enough to accommodate the town, machine and repair shops, and the steamboat landing. However, the irregular riverbank and the need for wide railyards with a long stretch of track for terminal facilities left little room for the town. It grew where it could on either side of the tracks. Glendive's northwest-southeast diagonal layout, platted by former army officer General Lewis Merrill of the Yellowstone Irrigation and Colonization Company and filed in 1882, causes confusion to this day. The side of town closest to the river came to be called the "north" side and that closest to the bluff the "south" side. Streets on the river half are designated "west" and on the bluff half, "east." Many streets and avenues were named for railroad and land company officials, a common practice of the time.

Glendive looked to a bright future in the summer of 1881, based on stock raising and agriculture, regional shipping via the railroad and river, and the operation of the railyard. An 1882 prospectus estimated that the railroad facilities and the operation of the railroad itself would provide steady employment for

The second Northern Pacific passenger depot, located on the east side of Merrill Avenue looking southwest, was constructed in 1882. Its second story was added in 1887. Fire destroyed the building in 1922. Courtesy FGM

The Northern Pacific roundhouse, completed circa 1882–83. The original building had eleven stalls, and eleven more increased its size in 1890. Over the years, more stalls accommodated the increase in traffic and larger ~~trains~~. Courtesy MHS Photo Archives *engines*

three hundred men who, with their families, were a ready-made population.

By 1883 Glendive had many single men, and boosters tried to discourage clerks, bartenders, and cashiers from coming to town; there were enough of those. Women, on the other hand, were scarce. In April of that year, the Glendive *Times* announced, "Glendive offers special inducements for domestic help. Girls for dining room work are in great demand at excellent wages. There is also a 'right smart' chance to catch on to husbands. Come along, girls."

The lower Yellowstone Valley proved exceptional for raising cattle, sheep, and horses in the 1880s and 1890s. The rapid rise of ranching added significantly to Glendive's growth. Small ranches began to dot the lower Yellowstone as early as the 1870s. Once buffalo no longer grazed in the region, stock, especially cattle, were brought into the area from as far away as Texas. Overstocking and the notorious winter of 1886–87 hit hard, dramatically reducing herds and ruining numerous local stockmen. Some, however, profited by acquiring land and the stock of ranchers facing financial ruin. Other stockmen diversified by raising sheep and hogs and by managing their cattle herds more conservatively. In 1889 the immense region that was the original Dawson County, an area the size of the state of Connecticut, supported a hundred thousand head of cattle and only three thousand people, many of whom lived in Glendive. (Between 1893 and 1919, ten new Montana counties and parts of counties were carved out of the original Dawson County.)

The arrival of the railroad in Glendive allowed the town to become a regional shipping point for livestock as well as a local supply and distribution center and county seat. Previously, most Montana cattle marketed out of state were driven *up ?*

down the river to Fort Custer and to the railhead at Pine Bluff near Cheyenne, Wyoming. Area ranchers like Charles Krug, George McCone, C. A. Thurston, and William F. Jordan became wealthy with the growth of the stock industry and subsequently became prominent Glendive businessmen. Likewise, some who came as businessmen, such as Henry Dion, G. D. Hollecker, and A. S. Foss, became major area stockmen. Many of these individuals played significant roles in community affairs and left a legacy of landmark buildings and homes.

Farming got a start in the open-range era, practiced mostly by area ranchers who grew hay and small plots of grain along stream bottoms and on the benchlands to feed their stock. In what would prove a cruel trick of nature, a period of above-average rainfall produced deceptively good crops. Local ranchers gave glowing testimonials that appeared in promotional literature, contributing to the rapid influx of homesteaders after 1900. Early ranchers practiced small-scale irrigation along streambeds, but several early movements successfully sought federal support for comprehensive irrigation projects in the lower Yellowstone Valley. In addition, there were ample coal reserves in the area. While of a lower grade than that used for locomotives, this locally available fuel source was marketed for heating area homes and businesses.

Despite its enthusiastic start, Glendive grew only gradually during the 1880s and 1890s. Its status as a division terminus, county seat, and local shipping and supply center provided a stable economic base. However, operation of the large ranches that spread over the Yellowstone Valley required comparatively few people.

The most vigorous growth during the late 1800s and early 1900s occurred on Glendive's west side, which included the early commercial blocks facing Merrill Avenue, the railroad

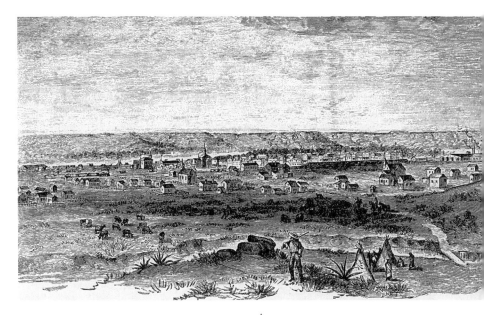

Glendive in 1885. From a sketch by | *The Northwest Magazine*, October
John Passmore, which appeared in | 1885. Courtesy MHS Library

facilities along the east side of the street, and the public buildings, residences, and liveries that crowded between Merrill
Avenue and the river. Construction of the Bell Street Bridge in
1896 and its reconstruction in 1902 made Bell Street a major
thoroughfare leading west from town and encouraged further commercial development along Merrill Avenue.

The Lower Yellowstone Irrigation Project, dryland farming, and an unusual amount of rainfall in the early 1900s altered the size and composition of the regional population. It
also affected the local economy and ushered in a new era,
transforming the town of Glendive into a city. The rapid increase in settlers to the Yellowstone Valley reduced the open
range and increased the number of farms, farmers, and agricultural products. These, in turn, increased the number of railroad branch and spur lines to towns such as Sidney and Circle.

New communities sprang up all along the way, including Jordan, Richey, Mondak, Lambert, Lindsay, Stipek, and Savage. Glendive's population nearly doubled to 2,600 between 1900 and 1910. By 1920, it had risen to 3,816.

Settlers realized from the beginning the necessity of irrigation if the lower Yellowstone River Valley was to be effectively farmed. Local ranchers and businessmen lobbied Congress for large, federally backed projects. Surveying projects in 1894 included a sixty-five-mile stretch for an irrigation canal twenty miles below Glendive to the confluence of the Yellowstone and Missouri rivers. Individuals also continued private irrigation without assistance. *Very few*

The Newlands Reclamation Act of 1902 brought the Lower Yellowstone Irrigation Project to eastern Montana. Forty surveyors mapped the lower Yellowstone Valley in 1904, and engineers planned construction of the project that began the following spring. By 1912, about 530 families had settled on some twenty-three thousand acres within the irrigation project. Altogether, the project watered approximately sixty-six thousand acres in Montana and North Dakota, making it one of America's most successful large-scale irrigation projects.

Supporters of the dryland farming movement maintained that it was impossible to irrigate more than a small percentage of the vast lands available for settlement. Dryland farming methods, such as deep plowing and soil compaction, could be used to farm nonirrigated land. The early success of farmers in the area and the steady espousal of the dryland farming theories of Hardy Webster Campbell and others temporarily dispelled the idea of the region as the "Great American Desert."

The Enlarged Homestead Act of 1909 offered homesteaders 320 acres of land, double the acreage previously allowed. As railroad companies completed their lines, they sold off huge

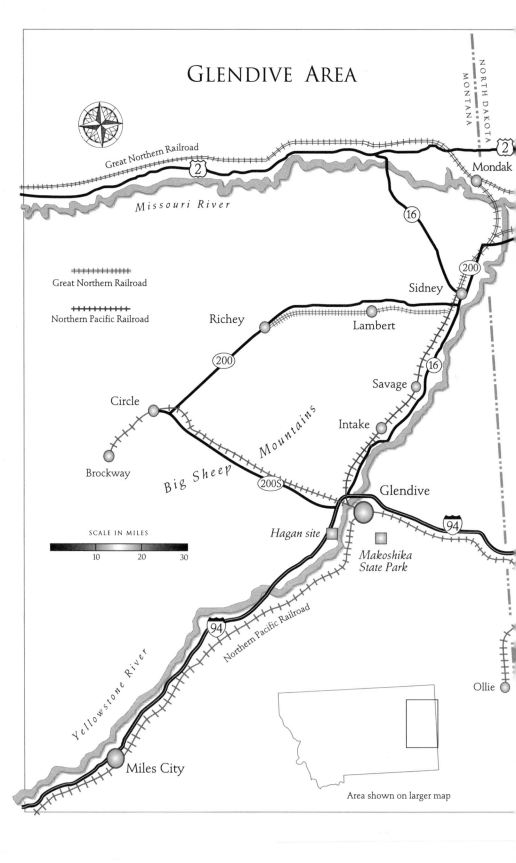

Glendive Area

unused tracts. Real estate schemes, railroad promotion, and land speculators, along with the dryland farming methods, enticed newcomers to the lower Yellowstone Valley, filling eastern Montana with first-time farmers working small parcels. Local and state organizations and agencies joined the promotional efforts. Immigrants came from a myriad of places, especially Scandinavia, by the trainload. Livestock continued to be important to the region, but farming had arrived as an area industry.

The population boom that came with the homesteaders accelerated construction of utilities, buildings, homes, sidewalks, and streets. Many of the business blocks, buildings, and residences that today comprise Glendive's historic streetscapes were built during this time period.

In 1890 public buildings clustered near the center of town on Merrill Avenue between Power and Mann streets. Expansion by the mid-1890s brought city buildings south to Williams Street and north to Valentine Street, primarily because of the Northern Pacific company housing. In 1905, these extended as far as Brennan and Raymond streets. By 1910, the division of the town into commercial, middle-class residential, and working-class residential neighborhoods was apparent.

Increased population placed additional pressure on Glendive's almost nonexistent infrastructure. In response, particularly to the need for a city water system, Glendive incorporated in 1902.

Prior to the completion of the municipal waterworks, some residents constructed windmills that pumped water to tanks in the upper stories of their homes for domestic use. Others made do with muddy water from the Yellowstone, hauled in wooden barrels to homes and businesses and sold for twenty-five cents a barrel. A resident who needed water put out a red flag, which

Glendive in the 1910s looking ⬦ includes the 1906 Lincoln School
northwest. Development of the east (**site 34**). Courtesy MHS Photo
side of town (in the foreground) Archives

visitors sometimes mistook for quarantine warnings. Barrels and
wells were, indeed, a source of epidemics, and Glendive desper-
ately needed a reliable, uncontaminated water supply. The town
was also beset with drainage problems. Streets were quagmires
after rainstorms, and basements frequently filled with water.

The first water system, built between 1905 and 1907, was
only a distribution system consisting of a pump station, a 250,000-
gallon settling pond, wooden water mains, and a hillside reser-
voir. A Wisconsin contractor, the only bidder on the project, built
the city sewerage at about the same time. Other improvements
during this period included cement sidewalks—the lack of which
had been the source of complaints since the beginning—and
graded and graveled streets. Paving began about 1920.

Power generation also improved with the construction of
a power-generating plant on Clough Street in 1899. It burned

the same year but was rebuilt and operating by 1900. In 1902, the attorney general of Dakota Territory received a franchise to construct an electric light plant, steam-heating system, and telephone exchange along the railroad right-of-way on Merrill Avenue at the end of Bell Street. Local businessmen constructed a new, larger power-generating plant on Clough Street in 1914.

The end of World War I brought crop failures and a drop in agricultural prices that hit hard. A combination of mother nature and the economy dealt lethal blows to many of the homesteaders who had flocked to the area. Inexperienced "honyockers" and the overly optimistic promotion of agricultural potential were only part of a larger problem. The end of higher-than-average rainfall exposed a basic truth: even 320 acres proved inadequate to make a living in eastern Montana, and most of the homesteaders were forced to abandon their dreams of farming the area. The Northern Pacific, however, offered economic stability to other segments of the population. In the 1920s, the Yellowstone Division employed two thousand people with an annual payroll of 3.6 million dollars; 1.5 million dollars of it went to employees in Glendive.

Agricultural conditions worsened during the Great Depression, and almost all of the homesteaders who had been able to hang on during the 1920s finally had to move on during the 1930s. The long-term sources of economic stability—the railroads and the ranches—also fell on hard times. Grain and beef prices fell, thousands of acres of land became tax delinquent, and land sold at sheriffs' sales for fifty cents to a dollar an acre.

The Great Depression did not, however, prove as disastrous to Glendive as it did to other areas in Montana. The Northern Pacific offices and shops, the town's history of economic stability, and its gradual economic growth buffered widespread adversity. Glendive proudly notes that it is the only Montana town where no banks failed during the Depression. The town's four banks survived because of Charles Krug's legendary vow not to let his own Merchants National Bank fail. Krug, Glendive's reputed first millionaire, pledged every penny of his own fortune to establish the confidence necessary to weather the storm.

Federal, state, and local organizations brought jobs to Glendive at the height of the Depression. Federal construction projects in the Glendive area included paving the Red Trail Highway between Bismarck and Billings and the construction of the Buffalo Rapids Irrigation Project between Glendive and Miles City. Local civic groups organized and lobbied for the Buffalo Rapids Irrigation Project, which was approved in 1937 and built by the Work Projects Administration between 1937 and 1940. Hundreds of workers excavated the thirty-five mile canal with four-horse teams. The main pumping plant, about twelve miles south of Glendive, served as the major staging area for the project.

In the last half of the twentieth century, the oil industry has become important to Glendive's economy, but the town's legacy of ranching and railroading is still part of its personality. As Glendive's history unfolds before the visitor through historic landmarks and gracious early homes, it should become evident that the town's story is still being written. Along its pleasant streets, newer buildings mingle with the old, a comfortable layering that reveals a town both proud of its past and enthusiastic about its future.

Main Street
of the Northwest

THE NORTHWEST MAGAZINE of August 1885 lamented that
"Glendive does not make a good showing of buildings for the
business that it does." There were two good reasons. A dispute
between the Yellowstone Land and Colonization Company and
the Northern Pacific Railroad over ownership of townsite lots, a
problem not completely resolved until 1896, was partly to blame.
Insecure titles compelled business owners to construct less per-
manent frame buildings instead of brick business blocks. The
railroad was the second reason for Glendive's poor commercial
buildings. Status as division headquarters demanded decent railroad facilities as a first priority. Bricks from Glendive's first brickyard all went to the Northern Pacific's building efforts.

Like all frontier towns that began with hastily constructed
wooden buildings, fire was a constant threat that plagued
Glendive from the very beginning. The town no doubt expe-
rienced earlier fires, but the first recorded one occurred in 1884
when a stove ignited the muslin that lined the rough interior
logs of a millinery shop. But when two different fires wiped
out more than thirteen businesses in 1886, it was the last straw.
There was no choice but to rebuild in something more sub-
stantial than wood. The earliest Glendive buildings date to
the time following those two conflagrations.

Henry Dion, who lost a saloon and mercantile to the first 1886 fire, finally constructed his own brick kiln so that he and his neighbors could build more fire-resistant buildings. Dion's was featured in the June 1889 issue of *The Northwest Magazine*, which readily acknowledged Glendive's recent cosmetic progress. Along with Dion's new business block, the town boasted a twenty-five-thousand-dollar brick county courthouse and a ten-thousand-dollar brick public school. Neither of these stand today, but Henry Dion's corner landmark (site 10) and several other business blocks (sites 9, 11, and 12) remain to represent the early period.

The Merrill Avenue Historic District, listed on the National Register of Historic Places, reflects the period from 1886 to 1930. Glendive's commercial district has historically been called the "Main Street of the Northwest" because it reflects the typical building patterns of most railroad towns along the western frontier. Styles and architectural elements discussed in this section can be found not just in Glendive but in many other towns across the northwest. Anchored on one end by the 1914 Neoclassical city hall (site 1), and on the other by the handsome 1922 Northern Pacific depot (site 14), the district encompasses buildings in the half blocks facing Merrill Avenue between Douglas and Clement streets. Commercial warehouses, terminals, lumberyards, and stockyards that once crowded the east side of Merrill Avenue and robbed the main street of its first bricks have long since been demolished, erasing the evidence of rail and river commerce that, along with ranching, was Glendive's early lifeblood. The commercial buildings on the west side today stand alone to tell the story of this once bustling part of town. The modern visitor can follow Glendive's trends and progress in the surviving mix of period buildings. The layering of architectural remodelings

Celebration in Glendive along Merrill Avenue, looking southwest about 1900. There is a distinct contrast between the older, drab frame build-

ings and the newer masonry business blocks with fancy ornamentation. The Yellowstone Hotel is at the extreme right. Courtesy FGM

reflects especially Italianate, Romanesque, and Neoclassical styles and later "polychrome," or multicolored, brick designs. Most of the Merrill Avenue buildings were constructed of locally produced brick, concrete block, and brick brought in by the railroad from Hebron, North Dakota.

The earliest Glendive buildings were built in Italianate and Gothic Revival styles. These styles were at the height of national fashion until about 1880, but remained popular in western commercial building through the 1880s and sometimes even later. Although no original facade has escaped remodeling entirely, the keen observer can spot tall, narrow, gently arched or rectangular windows in many of Glendive's surviving nineteenth-century buildings (sites 9, 10, 11, and 12). Characteristically Italianate features, windows such as these often

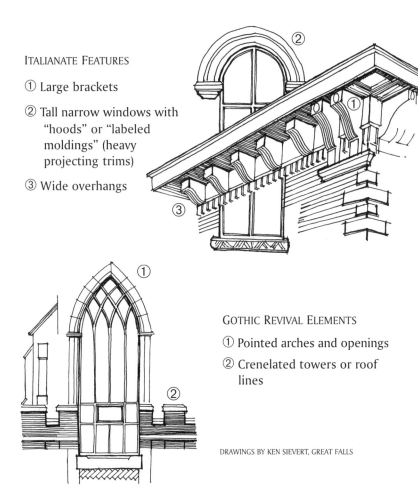

ITALIANATE FEATURES

① Large brackets

② Tall narrow windows with "hoods" or "labeled moldings" (heavy projecting trims)

③ Wide overhangs

GOTHIC REVIVAL ELEMENTS

① Pointed arches and openings

② Crenelated towers or roof lines

DRAWINGS BY KEN SIEVERT, GREAT FALLS

serve as the main clue to identifying the first historic layer in the earliest western commercial buildings. Wide, bracketed eaves, another major Italianate element, were usually the first thing to be remodeled. The growth of the railroad in the early 1880s helped promote Italianate architecture because decorative cast iron railings and other architectural embellishments could be shipped directly from foundries. A second early style, Gothic Revival, most commonly found today in church architecture, is characterized by pointed arches above windows and doorways and "crenelated" (notched like the tops of walls in medieval castles) towers or rooflines. Rare remnants of Gothic arches survive in the Henry Dion building (site 8).

A national trend in commercial architecture began with Boston architect Henry Hobson Richardson's adaptation of the Romanesque style in residential building in the 1870s. Rough-cut stone and round arches distinguish this style, which became popular across the United States in commercial and public buildings from the 1890s into the turn of the century. Glendive's architecture reflects this national trend, and Romanesque features, especially the characteristic round arches, can be seen in many of Glendive's earlier buildings (sites 4, 11, and 12).

The popularity of Neoclassical architecture can be directly attributed to the 1893 Columbian Exposition, the world's fair in Chicago, where temporary white pavilions with classical columns, arches, and domes charmed fairgoers. By 1900, most American towns had homes or buildings representing this style. The Neoclassical facades of architect Brynjulf Rivenes in particular mark the period from 1900 to 1920 in Glendive

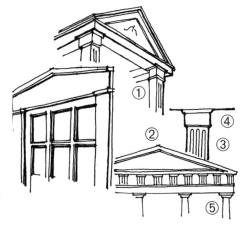

TYPICAL NEOCLASSICAL DETAILS

① Portico (porch)

② Triangular pediment

③ Pilasters (columns engaged in walls)

④ Capitals

⑤ Tall, light-colored columns

(sites 1, 5, 6, and 12). Although a number of the commercial buildings were probably designed by architects, only the works of this Norwegian-born, Miles City architect have been positively identified. Rivenes's symmetrically organized and finely detailed designs can be readily identified by their light-colored columns or pilasters (half columns attached to the building) with highly decorated capitals (tops) and intricate cornices (horizontal moldings at the top of the building).

Architecture of the 1920s and 1930s is also easy to recognize. Buildings of the later period are generally flatter and less flamboyant than their predecessors with "polychrome," or multicolored, brickwork as the main decorative element. Although these buildings are not as fancy as earlier commercial buildings, the nonetheless lively facades showcase the fine skills of local masons (sites 2, 3, and 4).

The commercial buildings that represent the period before 1900 reflect the architectural layering that characterizes most early buildings along American main streets, and all have important ties to Glendive founders involved in ranching, commerce, and the early community. One of these is the Douglas and Mead Company building at 119-121 North Merrill Avenue (site 12), originally two separate buildings constructed between 1886 and 1903. The 1903 remodel blended round, Romanesque arches above the entry and paired second-story windows with the building's original tall, narrow windows. Brynjulf Rivenes remodeled the entire facade in the Neoclassical style in 1915, redefining the pilasters with fancy capitals and adding a cornice with toothlike decoration called "dentils" at the roofline.

The Douglas and Mead Company conducted business on this corner from 1882 to the early 1950s. Henry F. Douglas, a merchant from Minneapolis, established stores near army posts in Montana and the Dakotas during the surveying and

In this circa 1905 photograph, the Merchants National Bank and the Douglas and Mead Company building (**site 12**) features a classic round-arched Romanesque-style entryway and round arches over paired second-story windows; its tall, narrow first- and second-floor single windows are characteristic of the Italianate style. Courtesy FGM

The Merchants National Bank and the Douglas and Mead Company building (**site 12**) after the 1915 remodeling by Brynjulf Rivenes. His redesign included a new entryway, prominent pilasters with capitals, and an elegant cornice. Although some of the second-story windows are today filled in, the arches remain visible, documenting change over time. Courtesy FGM

construction of the Northern Pacific Railroad. He formed Douglas and Mead Company with his brother-in-law David Mead in 1881 and was one of the cofounders of the Yellowstone Land and Colonization Company. David Mead was later president of the Merchants National Bank.

The Henry Dion family is well represented in the Merrill Avenue Historic District. Dion was the original owner of three of Glendive's landmark business blocks. The Dion building/ Exchange State Bank at 100-104 South Merrill Avenue (site 10), the Dion Brothers building at 106-108 South Merrill Avenue (site 9), and the Henry Dion building at 110 South Merrill Avenue (site 8) are all significant elements of the historic district. Merchant Henry Dion followed the construction of the Northern Pacific Railroad as it moved toward Glendive. He started a freight forwarding operation in 1879 and built a home and an office at the construction camp before the townsite was moved to its present location in 1881. After the fires of 1886, Dion built a brick Gothic Revival–style business block on South Merrill (site 10), where he engaged in the general mercantile business until he sold it to his sons, Fred and Harry, in 1908. Henry Dion was appointed the first sheriff of Dawson County by Territorial Governor Benjamin F. Potts in 1882, served as county treasurer, county commissioner, and longtime trustee of the Glendive schools. Dion was also president of the Exchange Bank, established in 1901, and remained president when the Exchange State Bank was founded in 1911. He died in 1920.

The Dion building/Exchange State Bank on the corner at 100-104 South Merrill (site 10), constructed after the fires of 1886, was extensively remodeled in 1929 by Glendive contractor John Holm. Originally Gothic Revival style, the building housed Dion's businesses on the street level, and the Glendive Club, the center of the town's social life, on the sec-

The three Dion buildings in the 100 block of South Merrill Avenue before remodeling. The Romanesque-Gothic Revival–style Dion building/Exchange State Bank in the foreground at 100-104 South Merrill Avenue (**site 10**) was radically remodeled in 1929. The Dion Brothers building at 106-108 South Merrill (**site 9**) carries the Neoclassical design imprint of Brynjulf Rivenes. The Henry Dion building to its left at 110 South Merrill Avenue (**site 8**) is similar in design to the original Dion building/ Exchange State Bank on the corner. Courtesy FGM

ond floor. *The Northwest Magazine* of June 1889 declared the club "a credit to Glendive to be able to maintain so attractive and well-managed an institution." An initiation fee of twenty-five dollars and ten dollars yearly dues entitled gentlemen members access to billiard and whist tables, magazines, news-papers, and lounging and smoking facilities. Ladies were al-lowed in the club one evening a week.

Henry Dion built the Dion Brothers building at 106-108 South Merrill (**site 9**) in stages between 1894 and 1910 to expand the family mercantile business that catered to area homesteaders. It is the best single example of commercial architecture in Glendive and dominates the block. Brynjulf Rivenes designed the splendid

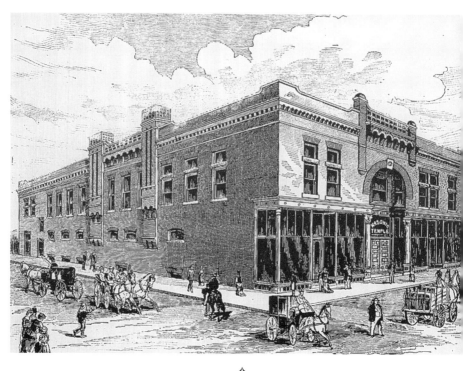

The original Masonic Temple building (**site 11**) as it appeared in the June 1889 issue of *The Northwest Magazine*. The large Romanesque-style arched entry was later remodeled and the narrow, Italianate windows enlarged. The original cornice at the roofline and tower-like pilasters on the building's south side have survived. Courtesy MHS Library

Neoclassical facade in 1910. It is an excellent example of Rivenes's favored Neoclassical design featuring brick and sand stone details, a splendid metal cornice and corner brick pilasters with decorative lions' heads. According to grandson Fred Dion, the lions' heads are a reminder that the French-Canadian name *Dion* was Americanized to rhyme with *lion*. Dion also built the Henry Dion building at 110 South Merrill Avenue (**site 8**) in 1905 as an investment. Romanesque and pointed Gothic Revival window arches, one of few such remaining examples in Glendive, highlight the fine detailing. Construction of the first water system was accomplished in 1906 and 1907 during Dion's term as mayor of Glendive, and a two-story addition constructed at the back of this commercial/residential building provided Dion's lucky tenants with the first running water and bathroom facilities in town.

The Masonic Temple building at 101 North Merrill (site 11) is one of Glendive's early buildings, constructed just after the Dion building and also featured in the June 1889 issue of *The Northwest Magazine*. A few original design features survive despite extensive remodeling in 1913. Glendive contractor Jerry Cain and Hoover and Spaulding of Minneapolis built the temple of local brick at a cost of $8,548. Upstairs, an opera house with a seating capacity of 179 was a welcome addition to Glendive society.

Romanesque-style arches, one of Glendive's most common early architectural elements, should by now be familiar to Glendive visitors. The Gillis-Foss building at 210-212 South Merrill Avenue (site 4), constructed between 1903 and 1905, features four semicircular Romanesque arches that highlight the second-story windows. Three tiers of multicolored brick define the arches. J. S. Gillis and photographer-turned-rancher A. S. Foss constructed the building, which originally housed a confectionery and a millinery. Like other two-part commercial buildings of the period, rental apartments were upstairs. Foss family members originally lived on the second floor of the southernmost building. Frank Kinney, a highly successful horse breeder and ferry operator, constructed the Kinney building at 222 South Merrill Avenue (site 2) in 1905. This building, like the Gillis-Foss building, showcases the attractive varied brickwork laid by Glendive masons during the busy homesteading period.

The Neoclassical style dominated Glendive's commercial streetscape during the period between 1900 and 1920 because of the influence of Brynjulf Rivenes, who designed many

Early streetscape looking north from the corner of South Merrill Avenue and West Power Street. The Kinney building (site 2) is at the extreme left and the Gillis-Foss building (site 4) to its right, center. Courtesy FGM

commercial, public, and residential buildings in eastern Montana. Rivenes designed the Rivenes-Wester building at 206 South Merrill Avenue (site 5) for his brother David's hardware business and the Krug building at 202 South Merrill Avenue (site 6), both between 1909 and 1910. Joseph L. Wester, an engineer for the Northern Pacific Railroad, built the two-part commercial buildings of poured concrete. The once-identical Neoclassical-style facades are not exactly identical today, but the prominent pilasters and decoratively carved capitals remain as evidence that they were a matched set.

Commercial buildings constructed or remodeled after 1910, except for those by Brynjulf Rivenes, are generally less grandly

Right to left are the striking Art Deco
Stipek building (site 7), the once-
twin Krug and Rivenes-Wester

buildings (sites 6 and 5), and the
Gillis-Foss building (site 4). Courtesy
SHPO

proportioned and have fewer embellishments. They include
one and two-story commercial blocks featuring multicolored
brickwork, contrasting stone trim, and modest decorative elements. Examples include two-part commercial blocks, such
as the Leidahl building at 218 South Merrill Avenue (site 3),
built in 1912, which reflects the simpler designs of this later
period. Although not as fancy as earlier buildings, it showcases the fine workmanship of local masons.

Commercial buildings on Bell Street constructed or remodeled during the 1920s and 1930s feature multicolored brick
and decorative concrete for stylistic effects. These include the
1886 Dion building/Exchange State Bank (site 10) that wraps
around the corner of Merrill and Bell and was remodeled in
1929. The two-story commercial building behind it was constructed at that time. The 1901 facade of the Stipek building
(site 7), at 200 South Merrill Avenue, was completely replaced

Brynjulf Rivenes designed the landmark Neoclassical-style Glendive City Hall (**site 1**) at the corner of South Merrill Avenue and West Power Street. Anchoring the upper end of the historic district, it is still used as Glendive's City Hall. Courtesy FGM

Glendive Post Office (**site 13**) financed by the Works Progress Administration in 1936. Courtesy FGM

in the late 1930s with Carrara glass (structural glass panels), glass block, heavy metal framed windows, a clipped (angled) corner entryway, and the word "Lulhaven" spelled out in neon. It is an outstanding representation of the Art Deco style, and the only one in the historic district. It is also the district's only contributing historic element dated after 1930.

Visitors can again appreciate the by now familiar work of Brynjulf Rivenes in the Glendive City Hall at the corner of South Merrill Avenue and West Power Street (site 1). Constructed in 1914 by Glendive contractor Wallace T. Perham, the building's Neoclassical design features include grandly proportioned columns, Ionic-style capitals, an elaborate cornice, and symmetrical elements.

The Works Progress Administration financed construction of the United States Post Office at the corner of Kendrick Avenue and Benham Street (site 13), outside the historic district but listed independently on the National Register. Glendive contractor John Sterhan built the seventy-thousand-dollar building which was patterned after standardized plans developed by the treasury department. Employees had barely moved into the new building in February 1936 when a natural gas explosion, according to the *Review*, left the building "wrecked almost beyond repair." John Sterhan again won the contract, and the entire southeast corner of the building had to be removed to repair the damage. The post office was reopened in October of that same year. The building displays quality materials and craftsmanship typical of federal construction projects during the Depression.

The river, the hills, and the railroad determined the layout of Glendive. As author Marian Place described it, the town grew "astraddle the tracks with its back toward the river and its face toward the soaring badlands." Glendive's west side is to the right of the tracks in the above photograph; the east side is to the left. Courtesy MHS Photo Archives

Residential Mosaic

━━━◆━━━

THE RAILROAD CUT a swath through the middle of Glendive, and the town from its beginning had to grow on either side. The two halves clearly reflect the personalities and livelihoods of their respective residents, although before the turn of the century the differences were not as clearly defined as they were later. The memoirs of early west side homeowner Elmer Herrick contain a partial explanation as to why Glendive's prosperous ranchers, professionals, and businessmen built their homes on that side of town. It seems that Montana's first attorney general, Henri Haskell, whom folks referred to as "the general," tried to persuade wealthy ranchers and stockmen moving into town at the turn of the century to buy his east side lots. Haskell was a brilliant attorney, but not known for his warm personality. Perhaps for this reason, Glendive newcomers opted for the west side "suburbs." They built a street named Meade Avenue and a disappointed Haskell later claimed that the land had been set aside for the likes of horse thieves. He afterward referred to Meade Avenue as "Horse Thief Row."

The west side did become the fashionable part of town. Architect-designed homes like Elmer Herrick's showplace (site 23), where even the children's playhouse had leaded glass windows, and Charles Krug's landmark mansion (site 20) reflected the tastes and social status of Glendive's most prominent citizens. Many homes had beautiful grounds with sweeping lawns ending at the riverbank. Later on, comparatively modest homes of the 1920s and 1930s gradually were built upon the once-extensive grounds of larger homes, reflecting a more conservative economy and producing a vintage mix of architectural styles.

Glendive's west side includes several distinct architectural styles as well as more modest, and less distinctive, types of early housing. A few examples of each will be mentioned here in detail, but there are others the visitor should be able to discover. The post-1930s homes found interspersed in the historic neighborhoods are beyond the scope of this guide.

The earliest homes in Glendive, in keeping with the national trend, are built in the rambling Queen Anne style that was the quintessential expression of the Victorian era, especially between 1880 and 1900. Queen Anne–style homes became popular throughout the United States through magazines, and by 1891 pattern book plans were readily available by mail for fifteen to twenty-five dollars. The Queen Anne

TYPICAL QUEEN ANNE FEATURES

① Irregular roofline/floorplan
② Towers, turrets
③ Wrap-around porches
④ Fancy trim
⑤ Decorative porch posts
and spindles

Many of Glendive's prominent citizens built residences near Bell Street. The Charles Krug mansion (**site 20**) is at the extreme left center. Many homes have either been moved or destroyed, including the Tom Lee residence in the lower left foreground, the Mead residence in the right foreground, the Henri Haskell residence across Bell Street from the Mead home, and the Henry Dion residence on Bell Street between the Haskell and the Krug residences. Courtesy FGM

hallmark is the irregularly shaped roofline and floor plan as well as the asymmetrical placement of windows and doors. Queen Anne houses display a wealth of textures and surfaces, including different types of decorative shingles and brick, wood, and stone in various combinations. Characteristic elements are wraparound porches, bay windows, turrets or towers, decorative turned wood posts and railing spindles, and "gingerbread" trim (**sites 18, 19, and 22**).

After the turn of the century, west side residents began to favor comfortable American four-square homes (**sites 15 and 16**) and elegant architect-designed Neoclassical-style residences (**sites 20 and 21**). From about 1900 to 1930, the American four-square enjoyed popularity across the country. So named for its boxy, square shape, four-square homes were economical to build with pattern book plans, although some are architect designed. Examples are common in virtually every American community. The shape lent itself to a simple floor plan of four equal-sized rooms on each of two stories. Glendive has its share of these easy-to-recognize homes, which usually have a one-story front porch and groups or pairs of evenly balanced windows. A bay window often projects from one side. Glendive also has some splendid examples of Neoclassical-style homes. Often architect designed, these were a by-product of the 1893 Columbian Exposition, which rekindled interest in classical architecture for commercial and residential buildings. The residential counterpart of this highly favored, elegant style includes the same tall, light-colored columns with fancy capitals, decorative cornices, and symmetry that highlight Neoclassical commercial buildings.

The railroad inspired a new era of "folk housing" that made the sod, log, and heavy hewn-timbered homes of prerailroad days quickly obsolete. Materials and prefabricated light framing could easily and cheaply be shipped by rail. Interestingly, however, folk shapes (like that derived from the most primitive log cabin) persisted. The simple gable-front (site 23 is an elegant example) can be either one or two stories, with the peak of the roof facing the front. The gable-front-and-wing (like the gable-front, but with an addition on one side) are commonly found as modest workers' homes and company tract housing, especially in western railroad towns like Glendive (sites 17 and 26). Depending on the size and the type of trim, gable-front houses range from very simple to fairly elaborate. It is this type of housing that bridges the east and west sides in Glendive since the gable-front is found in both neighborhoods in various sizes and settings.

By the turn of the century, the east side's working-class character had been well established, but in the early days, a few of Glendive's leading citizens built fine homes in that part of town. The area grew slowly, however, and its early character was less defined. Harry Johnson, a Northern Pacific Railroad employee who came to Glendive in 1883, remembered few buildings on the east side at that time and that it was an "open prairie used for picketing horses and herding cows." The Northern Pacific section house at 205 East Power and the superintendent's house at 303 South Nowlan (site 25) were constructed in 1884. Still, east side construction lagged behind the rest of the town, and even by 1903 most of the houses were confined to Valentine Street.

Eventually, the working backbone of Glendive settled on the east side. Residents of Scandinavian, Italian, and German origins who came to Glendive to work for the railroad lived on the east side, as did clerks and neighborhood shopkeepers and other blue-collar workers. North on Sargent, "little Italy" was home to the families of grocer Joe Crisafulli, shoemaker Dominic Giarrantana, and others whose ethnic heritage and colorful speech enriched the community.

Churches, too, enlivened both west and east side streetscapes. The Methodist Episcopal Church was built upon the west side in the heart of its congregation (site 30). On the east side, the Zion Lutheran Church of Glendive (site 29) speaks to the town's large Scandinavian population. Glendive's first Catholic church, St. Juliana's, was established on the east side of town in 1886 in a church purchased from the Congregationalists. When the congregation outgrew the building, Catholics constructed the west side Sacred Heart Church (site 31), completed in 1926.

The Henry Dion home (site 19) is a grand example of the Queen Anne style with its uneven roofline and fancy gingerbread trim. The family reportedly enlarged the house with the birth of each new member. Courtesy MHS Photo Archives

WEST SIDE HOMES

The west side's most distinguished early homes were located along West Bell and West Towne streets, immediately adjacent to the historic city center. Some have been demolished or moved while others have undergone various alterations but stand as reminders of the many landmark residences that once graced this part of town.

The Queen Anne–style residences of Henry Dion at 414 West Towne Street (site 19) and G. D. Hollecker at 201 River (site 18) reflect Victorian-era taste before the turn of the century. Irregular lines, bay windows, and wraparound porches are the hallmarks of this architectural style preferred during the 1880s and 1890s.

The Dion home is one of the earliest in the area. Henry Dion came to Glendive just before the railroad in 1881. His varied career included supervising the building of Fort Lincoln in Dakota Territory in 1872 and freighting supplies between Miles City and the gold camps in the Black Hills. Initially a small house, the Dion residence was constructed in stages from the 1880s until 1910. The sprawling Queen Anne–style home was moved from its original location on Bell Street to its present site in the 1960s.

The George D. Hollecker residence at 201 River Avenue (site 18) was constructed in 1897 by local contractor J. A. Morse. Hollecker, a prominent merchant and rancher who raised purebred cattle, race horses, and Shetland ponies, brought his family to Glendive in the 1890s when the town offered few amenities.

The Queen Anne home of merchant and rancher G. D. Hollecker at 201 River Avenue (**site 18**), constructed in 1897, featured an upstairs billiard room and inviting wraparound porch. Courtesy SHPO

The Charles Krug residence at 103 North Douglas Street (**site 20**) is considered by many Glendive's most prominent historic residence. An outstanding example of Neoclassical architecture, the design shows the strict symmetry, a grand columned entryway, and elegantly ornamented cornice characteristic of the style. Courtesy FGM

An 1885 article in *The Northwest Magazine* reported that "Cattle owners have no use for drunken desperadoes" and "the wild cowboy of the plains is fast becoming extinct." The Holleckers, however, found quite the contrary when they arrived on the Fourth of July in 1894. There was such boisterous riding, shooting, and drinking by local cowboys that Mrs. Hollecker got back on the train with three-year-old Jessie and six-week-old Marie and went home to her mother's until proper housing could be secured. The Holleckers built this landmark home a few years later.

The best-known historic residence in Glendive is that of Charles Krug, Glendive rancher, banker, and civic leader, who had the residence at 103 North Douglas Street (**site 20**) constructed for his large family in 1907. The twenty-five-room Neoclassical-style mansion was designed by architect Herbert C. Chivers of St. Louis. Built of glazed Hebron, North Dakota,

The American four-square Miskimen residence at 211 West Towne Street (**site 15**) was designed by Brynjulf Rivenes, revealing the architect's ability to employ styles other than the Neoclassical. Courtesy SHPO

brick and limestone, the interior is elaborately and elegantly finished. Intricately carved oak columns, elaborate stairwork and corner fireplaces with decorative glazed porcelain tile are fitting accoutrements for Glendive's reputed first millionaire. A merry-go-round in the basement was the envy of neighborhood children. Work with the Northern Pacific brought Krug, a native of Ohio, to Glendive in 1881. Krug's sister Emma, a dressmaker, came west with him hoping the climate would relieve her asthma. Krug lost his hard-earned herd of cattle in the disastrous winter of 1887 and then turned to sheep, becoming the largest sheep rancher in eastern Montana. He was also a founder and president of the Merchants National Bank. At one time Krug owned fifty-four sections of land. The home is listed on the National Register of Historic Places.

The west side includes several exceptional examples of American four-square homes built between 1900 and 1920. The Miskimen residence at 211 West Towne Street (**site 15**), designed by Brynjulf Rivenes, proves that this fine architect worked well with styles other than the Neoclassical, for which he is best known. The home was constructed in 1909 by J. H. Miskimen as a surprise for his wife, Nellie. Dr. Miskimen was an optometrist, jeweler, photographer, realtor, and insurance agent, as well as Glendive's first mayor and a founder of the First National Bank.

The Blackstock residence at 217 West Towne Street (**site 16**), built circa 1905–10 and listed on the National Register of Historic Places, is another excellent example of the American four-square. Likely constructed from pattern book plans, its boxy shape, front porch spanning the front, and side bay window are classic four-square elements.

The National Register–listed Blackstock residence at 217 West Towne Street (**site 16**) is an excellent example of the basic American four-square residence. Likely constructed from pattern book plans, it sports the four-square's characteristically boxy shape. Courtesy SHPO

The McCone residence at 218 West Towne (**site 17**) is a modest gable-front-and-wing cottage, a simple house form that bridges the east and west sides. The peak of the gable faces front, while an addition to the side creates an "L" shape and allows for a small porch. Courtesy SHPO

The modest gable-front-and-wing cottage of George McCone, one of Glendive's pioneers, was built between 1893 and 1903 at 218 West Towne Street (**site 17**). It is listed on the National Register of Historic Places. A native of New York, McCone was a cattleman who arrived in the Glendive area in 1882. He later served in the state house of representatives and the senate, where he sponsored the McCone Act enabling the organization of new counties by popular vote. McCone County, created in 1919, is named after him.

Many of Glendive's landmark residences were built along North Meade and North Kendrick avenues as the west side residential district leapfrogged north about 1905 into the pasture of Judge Allen's old homestead, upsetting Henri Haskell's hopes for east-side development. The area today remains free of commercial encroachment. Many residents were area ranchers who moved to town after the turn of the century for better access to their businesses and so that their children could attend school.

The core of the Meade Avenue landmark homes includes those of William F. Jordan, Thomas F. Hagan, and Elmer Herrick, all of which boast distinctive architectural styles and spacious, well-kept grounds. When the William F. Jordan home at 707 North Meade (**site 22**) was constructed in 1901, it stood alone in the stately "suburbs," where Glendive's other prominent citizens were soon to follow. Jordan, a Texan, started out in the livestock business. He married May Miller, who, according to family legend, brought her three small daughters by steamboat to Fort Keogh in 1876. She was looking for her first husband, a sutler in the army, who had somehow lost touch with his family. Whether she found him is a mystery, but Miller ended up working in a hotel in Miles City. After she married William Jordan, the couple established the landmark Jordan Hotel in

North Meade Avenue looking northeast circa 1910. The Neoclassical Thomas Hagan residence (**site 21**) is in the left foreground, with the Queen Anne William Jordan residence (**site 22**) and the gable-front Elmer Herrick residence (**site 23**) behind it. Courtesy FGM

The William F. Jordan home at 707 North Meade Avenue (**site 22**) was once far removed from the other residences in town. A fence originally separated the yard from the prairie that became Meade Avenue. Courtesy FGM

1901. The Jordans' residence is one of the best examples of Queen Anne residential architecture in Glendive. Its uneven roofline, fish-scale shingles, bay windows, and "eyebrow" dormer are typical Queen Anne elements.

Unlike most of Glendive's leading citizens, Thomas F. Hagan, who resided at 621 North Meade Avenue (**site 21**), was a college graduate. He came to Glendive in 1884 as a fireman with the railroad and soon acquired the Pabst Beer distributorship. He also raised horses and cattle, helped found the Glendive First National Bank and the Jordan Hotel Company, and served as mayor from 1909 to 1915. Hagan's grand Neoclassical-style home was designed by renowned St. Paul architect Cass Gilbert and built in 1905. The building materials came all the way from Chicago. The home features a centered entry with full-length columns and Ionic capitals, graceful porches, and a richly detailed roof. A widow's walk, accessed

The Thomas F. Hagan residence at 621 North Meade Avenue (**site 21**) is one of Glendive's two landmark Neoclassical-style residences. A wrought iron fence once enclosed part of the property, which extended to the Yellowstone River. Courtesy FGM

The gable-front residence of Elmer Herrick at 717 North Meade Avenue (**site 23**) is an elegant example of this traditional house form. Courtesy FGM

through attic stairs, originally afforded stunning views of the surrounding countryside.

The Elmer Herrick residence at 717 North Meade Avenue (**site 23**) was built between 1907 and 1908 after the Herricks sold their ranch and moved to town. The home is a striking and elaborate example of a gable-front residence with a spacious wraparound front porch, Ionic columns, and two-story bay windows. The Herricks' lawn originally extended to the Yellowstone River. A self-made horse breeder, cattle and sheep rancher, Herrick became vice president of the Exchange Bank, helped organize the First State Bank of Wibaux, and served on the Glendive City Council.

The Parsonage of the First Methodist Episcopal Church at 209 North Kendrick (**site 30**) is a fine example of the Craftsman bungalow, the preferred middle-class American house

The Craftsman style, preferred by middle-class homeowners from about 1910 to the 1930s, was chosen for the 1913 Methodist Episcopal Parsonage (**site 30**). Courtesy SHPO

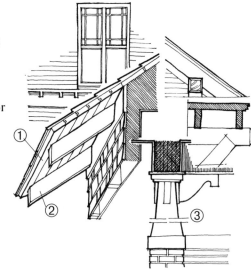

TYPICAL CRAFTSMAN FEATURES

① Wide overhanging eaves

② Exposed rafters

③ Heavy squared columns or porch supports

style from 1910 to the 1930s. Characterized by wide over-hanging eaves with exposed rafters, heavy squared columns, natural colors, and a flared roof, the 1913 parsonage is listed on the National Register as companion to the church. Another fine Craftsman home is the Wallace T. Perham residence at 812 North Kendrick (**site 24**, not pictured).

EAST SIDE HOMES

Significant residences on the east side of town include those associated with the Northern Pacific Railroad and with individuals who played a role in the development of Glendive. The Northern Pacific Railroad built a home at 303 South Nowlan (**site 25**) in 1884 for its superintendent, who had been unable to find suitable housing. The railroad's building and bridge crew built the residence using railroad ties in several places for support beams. Constructed of the earliest locally made brick, the home cost thirteen hundred dollars to build, a tidy sum in the 1880s. Innovative indoor plumbing—the

Railroad superintendent's residence at 303 South Nowlan looking east (**site 25**). Characteristic of the 1880s, the gable-front-and-wing residence has Italianate details above the windows and a beautiful two-story front porch. The residence is flanked by other side-gabled railroad workers' cottages constructed at the same time. Photograph taken in 1884. Courtesy FGM

water was pumped in by a windmill—and a graceful circular staircase set this refined two-story residence apart. The Northern Pacific owned the house until 1953.

In 1903, in response to continued housing shortages in Glendive for railroad employees, especially machinists, the Northern Pacific contracted with Fred Birch and W. H. Lee to build ten identical railroad company homes on East Valentine Street and South Sargent Avenue according to plans prepared by the railroad. Six of these, now privately owned, are still standing at 307-321 East Valentine (**site 26**). An early photograph reveals that these homes did not originally have bathrooms; there is a row of identical outhouses in the backyards. The houses, all 1½ story gable-front-and-wing with horizontal clapboard siding, were constructed with wood sills resting on wood blocks. Each was furnished with water from the railroad water tank near the roundhouse. The residence at 321 East Valentine Street has the best design and materials integrity of the houses remaining.

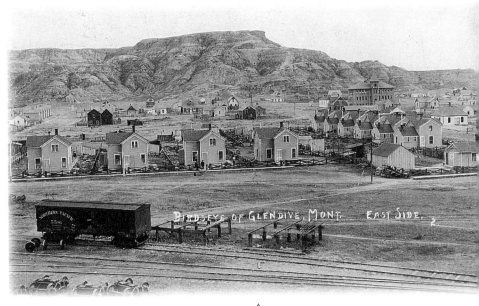

Railroad company houses on the east side of town photographed in 1914 looking south. The homes facing the camera are located on South Sargent Avenue and the residences to the right face East Valentine Street with Lincoln School (**site 34**) in the background. Courtesy MHS Photo Archives

The Martin Norderud residence at 523 East Towne Street (site 27, not pictured) is representative of carpenter-built gable-front-and-wing workers' cottages found on the east side. Fish-scale shingles and spindled porch supports reveal affinities with the Queen Anne style and a spark of individuality. Norderud was a railway worker who came to Glendive from Norway to join an uncle. Norderud bought the house in 1909 for twenty-five dollars.

The cottage of C. S. Thorpe, reverend of the Zion Lutheran Church, is a simple side-gabled residence with a front porch at 217 South Sargeant Avenue, and except for its newer siding, it appears much as it did in the early 1900s (**site 28**, not pictured). Thorpe left a fascinating portrait of turn-of-the-century Glendive in a series of letters to his family, published in *Montana The Magazine of Western History*, winter 1974.

CHURCHES

Churches are important elements of the residential street-scapes of both the west and east sides. The Zion Lutheran Church of Glendive at 320 East Power Street (**site 29**) is one of the most architecturally significant buildings on the east side of the tracks and, along with the C. S. Thorpe and Martin Norderud homes, is symbolic of the importance of Scandinavians, especially Norwegians, in the settlement of Glendive. Newly ordained Reverend Thorpe traveled among seven eastern Montana and western North Dakota counties to preach sermons in Norwegian and English to his far-flung parishioners. Thorpe's home base was in Glendive during the construction of this Gothic Revival–style church, built between

The Zion Lutheran Church of Glendive (**site 29**) at 320 East Power Street was built between 1907 and 1908. This church stands as a symbol of the importance of Norwegian settlement on Glendive's east side and of the contribution made by church architecture to the city's built environment. Courtesy SHPO

1907 and 1908 by Schloss Construction. Like all of Glendive's historic churches, it features multicolored brickwork similar to that seen in the town's twentieth-century commercial buildings. A square bell tower and the beautiful pointed-arch windows are hallmarks of the Gothic style.

The most architecturally significant churches on the west side of town are the National Register–listed First Methodist Episcopal Church at 209 North Kendrick (site 30) and the Sacred Heart Church at 316 West Benham Street (site 31), both designed by Brynjulf Rivenes. Wallace T. Perham built the English Gothic–style First Methodist Episcopal Church in 1909. Notable design features include the crenelated (notched-edge) bell tower, pointed arches, and multicolored brickwork. The Sacred Heart Catholic Church (site 31) was built by local contractor John Holm between 1925 and 1926 at a cost of fifty thousand dollars. The church, built in a mixed style reminiscent of Early Italian Christian and Romanesque architecture, dominates the corner of Benham Street and Meade Avenue.

Brynjulf Rivenes, most noted for his Neoclassical-style buildings, designed the English-Gothic First Methodist Episcopal Church (site 30). Built by Wallace Perham, the design features pointed arch windows and a crenelated bell tower. Courtesy SHPO

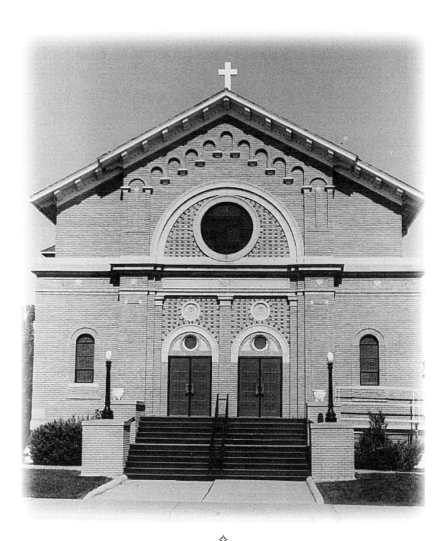

Patterns of tan Hebron brick and red brick highlight the facade of the 1926 Sacred Heart Catholic Church (**site 31**) designed by Brynjulf Rivenes. Bishop Mathias Lenihan donated the rose window, which bears his coat of arms and motto "Fides et Caritas" (Faith and Charity). Courtesy SHPO

The square bell tower, rose window above the main entrance, and magnificent brickwork make this church an integral, significant west side landmark. The tan-colored brick was shipped in from Hebron, North Dakota.

SCHOOLS

Lincoln School, Washington School, Dawson County High School, and Dawson Community College document the high regard city founders had for education. Area ranchers built homes in Glendive so they could send their children to city and county schools. In addition, the Glendive Woman's Club secured space for a volunteer public library in the basement of the new City Hall in 1915. Volunteers ran the library until it became part of city government in 1923. The city's several public librarians then contributed immeasurably to Glendive's role as a center of education in eastern Montana. The Lincoln School (**site 34**), located on Nowlan Avenue between East Power and East Valentine streets, was built in 1906. Wallace T. Perham combined narrow, Italianate-style windows and other Italianate details with a Romanesque arched entry, reflecting the earlier architecture seen in the commercial district. Combinations reviving styles fashionable in the previous century are found in many other early commercial and public buildings in Glendive. Dawson County High School (**site 33**) was another Italianate-style building constructed in 1908 on Merrill Avenue between West Slocum and West Allard streets, but was destroyed by a fire in 1966. Washington School (**site 32**), built of brick in 1914 on River Avenue between West Borden and West Dodge streets, has less pronounced design features, but is a major structure that cost fifty thousand dollars to build.

Lincoln School (**site 34**) on Nowlan Avenue between East Power and East Valentine streets features narrow Italianate-style windows and a Romanesque-arched entryway. The appearance of the school has changed through several additions and remodelings. Courtesy FGM

The Glendive Milling Company flour mill on Clough Street between West Valentine and West Bell streets (**site 39**). Courtesy FGM

What Made
Glendive Run

GLENDIVE WAS BORN for the railroad and fueled by the stock industry, and transportation and agricultural commerce kept Glendive going despite the fires, drought, Depression, and two world wars that spelled disaster for many other small Montana towns. Key infrastructure that supported the town's continued existence include the Bell Street Bridge, Northern Pacific depot, pedestrian underpass, settling ponds, and water treatment plants. Other industrial components, including the many railroad-related facilities, freight yards, stockyards, and early power facilities that once dominated the city's landscape, have been consigned to memory. A few remaining buildings, such as the roundhouse and machine shops on the east side of town, are difficult to access and view. Even the Bell Street Bridge, which played such a vital role in the life of the city, is now closed to traffic. The massive Glendive Heat, Light, and Electric Plant, which once supplied power to the city and steam heat to the city's businesses, has been demolished and so have most remnants of the once-spirited steamboat landing. Enough remains, however, to provide insight into what once made Glendive run.

Two other bridges linked Glendive to points north before the Bell Street Bridge (site 35) spanned the Yellowstone's muddy waters in 1926. Although Glendive was an important shipping and distribution center, the river made access from the northwest difficult in the early days. In the early 1890s, Frank Kinney's ferry transported people and goods back and forth as long as the weather permitted. But during periods of high water and ice breakup, crossing was treacherous. Businessmen favored building a bridge, but the big cattlemen resisted the idea partly because of taxes and partly for fear that the bridge would encourage competitive small-time cattlemen, called "nesters." After years of debate, Dawson County constructed the first bridge across the Yellowstone at Glendive in 1895. Floods and an ice jam destroyed the bridge and took twelve lives in 1899; it was rebuilt in 1902. The present Bell Street Bridge was built in 1926 alongside the old bridge, which was later dismantled.

The Bell Street Bridge represents a crucial link to travel and commerce and serves as a reminder of the time and effort made to keep this corridor open. This bridge, unlike its predecessors, was designed to accommodate automobile traffic. Boomer, McGuire, and Blakesly of Great Falls built the bridge with federal and county funds, totaling more than $300,000, under the auspices of the Montana State Highway Commission. The construction of the riveted steel Warren through-truss bridge is characterized by the "W" configuration made by its diagonal members and above-roadway trusswork. The Bell Street Bridge, listed on the National Register, is one of the longest of its kind in Montana and represents a significant engineering accomplishment.

Glendive's most significant remaining railroad-related building is the Northern Pacific Railroad Depot (site 14), constructed in 1922, which today marks the upper end of the Merrill Avenue Historic District. The first depot, built in 1882,

The Bell Street Bridge (**site 35**), constructed in 1926 at a cost of over $300,000, was designed to accom- modate automobile traffic and to keep an important historic travel corridor open to the north. Courtesy FGM

had served the town well and witnessed many changes in rail-road technology. When the 1882 depot was built, freight trains traveled ten miles per hour, and two brass-trimmed engines weighing 31 tons each were the pride of the line. The crew made frequent stops along the way to hunt prairie chickens, ducks, deer, and an occasional buffalo. When fire destroyed the first depot and the present building replaced it in 1922, passenger trains weighed 157 tons and traveled eighty miles an hour.

The new depot and headquarters for the Northern Pacific Yellowstone Division cost over $200,000 to build. Northern Pacific architect O. M. Rognan designed the three-story build-ing, constructed by the Winston-Grant Company, the largest railroad and building contractor in the northwest at that time.

The Northern Pacific Railroad depot (site 14) was constructed in 1922 to house offices of the Yellowstone Division, which, at that time, extended from Mandan, North Dakota, to Billings, Montana. Courtesy FGM

In addition to division administrative offices and passenger facilities, a large lunchroom served the traveling public and crews. Because the railroad did not want to use city water for its boilers and shops for fear of becoming a "captive" customer of the city, it built a water treatment plant in the new depot basement in 1929.

Accidents involving trains and pedestrians had always been a public concern. The Northern Pacific finally responded by building the pedestrian underpass joining the east and west sides of town at Power Street (site 36). Joseph L. Wester, foreman for the Northern Pacific bridge and building department, constructed the underpass under trying conditions, including frequent flooding, in the winter of 1914. Concrete forty inches thick braced the tunnel to withstand the weight exerted by trains overhead.

The National Register–listed Northern Pacific settlement ponds (site 37) behind the city water treatment plant at 420 West Bell Street (site 38) are visual reminders of the difficulty that the Northern Pacific Railroad had in obtaining water pure enough for its steam locomotive boilers. The Northern Pacific built these ponds between 1905 and 1910 near a pump and well close to the Yellowstone River. One pump sent water from the river to the tanks and another pumped water from the ponds to the railroad shops and water towers in the railyards. The covered tanks were later converted into city maintenance shops.

The Northern Pacific was a good partner to Glendive, particularly in the matter of fire fighting. From the earliest days, the railroad provided much of the fire-fighting equipment and residents depended upon the railyard whistles to sound the alarm in case of fire. After the turn of the century, city and

The city of Glendive water treatment plant, built between 1916 and 1917 at 420 West Bell Street (**site 38**), resulted from years of debate and struggle to obtain a reliable water supply. Courtesy FGM

railroad officials made a joint plan. The city provided the equipment (purchased at cost through the Northern Pacific) and the railroad built the fire station and fire plugs along its water supply lines.

The National Register–listed water treatment plant (site 38) at 420 West Bell Street was the city's solution to the water supply and quality problems that it had struggled with from the beginning. After it became apparent that a water distribution system constructed in 1905–7 was insufficient to end its water quality problems, the city hired the engineering firm of Burns and McConnell in 1916 to design a water filtration plant. Northwood Engineering Company of Florence, Massachusetts, built the plant between 1916 and 1917 at a cost of $32,610. A water softening plant, designed by city engineer C. W. Eyer in 1934 and said to have been the first in Montana, was financed through a $15,000 bond issue and a $19,000 federal grant through the Works Progress Administration. Modernization and expansion occurred in 1941 and 1960, but the original sections of the building remain in use. They represent the most controversial and expensive project undertaken by Glendive and the foresight of its city officials.

The Glendive Milling Company flour mill located on Clough Street between Valentine and Bell streets represents the historic importance of agriculture to the Glendive-area economy and a local attempt to base an industry on it (site 39). The company was incorporated in 1917 and had a board of directors consisting of local businessmen Charles Krug, Frank Kinney, and F. C. Hughes and two Billings businessmen. However, the mill was not a successful operation and was purchased outright by Charles Krug in 1924. It was later owned by several parties, greatly enlarged and converted to a feed production plant.

Glendive Today

SEVERAL BOOM PERIODS since the 1930s temporarily increased the size of Glendive and dramatically affected its historic landscape. The increase in railroad business during World War II brought new prosperity. Above-average rainfall between 1941 and 1944 was a surprise bonus, and area farmers set production records that recalled the homestead boom of the teens. Shortly after the war, the railroad remodeled and enlarged its shops, and Montana–Dakota Utilities made Glendive its distribution center. F. T. Reynolds built grocery stores and a warehouse in Glendive, and the Glendive Stock Sales Company established what was to be a highly successful stock sales yard on Sargent Street in 1947. The Montana Department of Transportation also located its eastern headquarters in Glendive. During the late 1940s, banks, automobile dealership, and implement companies all constructed new buildings in the town.

Between 1950 and 1960, Glendive's population increased significantly because of oil discoveries in the Williston Basin in the Dakotas and Montana. Almost thirty million barrels of oil were produced in the area between 1951 and 1976, and Glendive served as a staging area for major oil companies. As a result, population rose from five thousand to seven thousand and Glendive sprouted several new neighborhoods including

Glendive Manor to the southeast, Prospect Heights on the upper north end, and the Hillcrest addition to the northeast. The commercial district grew as well, and new construction in the 1950s included a grain elevator on Merrill Avenue north of the railroad depot. Several new banks and a telephone company building dramatically altered the appearance of the central business district just west of Merrill Avenue. Notable additions to the town's cultural and historic landscape in the 1960s include construction of the Frontier Gateway Museum, renovation of the high school, and a new campus for Dawson Community College.

The 1960s oil boom marked the peak of Glendive's population, and by 1990, the population had dropped to approximately pre-World War II levels, although oil continues to contribute significantly to the area economy. So, too, do older sources of jobs: agriculture and county government. These are increasingly supplemented by tourism as people continue to discover the area's fascinating history, natural beauty, and sporting possibilities. At heart, however, Glendive remains an agricultural railroad town, the rich heritage of its origins clearly laid across the landscape and embedded in the spirit of the community.

Afterword

BY LOUISE CROSS

Curator of the Frontier Gateway Museum

LIKE MOST SMALL Montana towns, Glendive finds itself in some-what of a dilemma. How can the town move with the times, look forward and prepare for the twenty-first century, and yet retain the flavor and color of its history? Straddling the present, Glendive struggles to keep one foot in the past while placing the other firmly in the future. This is not always a comfortable position.

Awareness of the benefits of historic preservation has existed in Glendive for some time. As early as 1985, plans were set in motion to develop a downtown historic district. Working with the State Historic Preservation Office and innumerable volunteers, chief investigator Bill Babcock of Missoula surveyed every building in the proposed district, which included all of the town's main street, Merrill Avenue, from Douglas to Clement streets. The completed 1987–88 survey reported that in the mortar and bricks of Glendive's buildings was a story to be told and saved.

The survey was an eye-opener for local residents—not only for newcomers but also for descendants of pioneer families. It revealed how closely the present was linked to the past. Of the initial two dozen buildings submitted to the governor's preservation review board, nine were accepted for the National Register. Each of these buildings designated as "historic" had played a significant role in what modern Glendive has become.

Unfortunately, in the effort to meet the demands of a modern rural society, some of the historic buildings have been altered. Ornate fronts on buildings in the business district have given way to more utilitarian material. Tall, narrow windows have bowed to the requirements of energy efficiency and have been shortened or covered.

Yet landmark residences of distinctive architectural style have, for the most part, retained their integrity. And, in a few cases even the original interiors have been restored. The Krug home, a Neoclassical mansion, has retained its original interior and exterior design, although it is now a bed and breakfast, not a private residence. The Bell Street Bridge, slated for demolition, was rescued by the Bell Street Bridge Historical Committee in 1992 and has been converted to a pedestrian and bicycle trail over the Yellowstone River.

Changes are part of the fabric of life. No one or no place is immune to them. Many can be beneficial if undertaken with an understanding of what a community has been and what it wants to become. There is no reason why the present cannot mesh with the past and still prepare for the next century.

Glendive Time Line

74 MILLION B.P. Start of formation of badlands and Makoshika State Park

11,500 B.P. Evidence of first human habitation near Glendive

1650 Approximate date of Hagan archeological site habitation

1800 Glendive area inhabited by Crows, Assiniboines, and Blackfeet

1805 Antoine François Larocque explores lower Yellowstone

1806 Captain William Clark camps at Glendive Creek, August 1

1855–60 Lieutenant Governor K. Warren and Captain William F. Raynolds map the lower Yellowstone River

1865 Harney–Sanborn Treaty of 1865 recognizes Glendive area as Sioux Land

1868 Treaty of Fort Laramie reaffirms Glendive area as Sioux but provides for railroad right-of-way

1869 Dawson County created on January 15

1873 General Forsyth establishes Camp Canby

1881 First train arrives in Glendive on July 5

1882 Original townsite platted; Glendive established as county seat for Dawson County

1886 Fire destroys thirteen businesses in 100 Block of South Merrill Avenue in March

1889 Montana becomes a state; Henri Haskell of Glendive appointed first attorney general

1889 Glendive Electric Light Company constructs a power-generating plant on Clough Street

1895 Construction of first Bell Street Bridge

1900 Glendive population is 1,435; that of Dawson County is 2,443

1902 City of Glendive incorporates on October 6. J. H. Miskimen is elected first mayor

1904 Lower Yellowstone Irrigation Project authorized

1909 Fort Peck Indian Reservation opened to settlement; commencement of homestead era

1910 Glendive population is 2,600; that of Dawson County is 12,725

1914 Pedestrian underpass joins west and east sides of town

1920 Glendive population is 3,816, that of Dawson County is 9,239

1926 Present Bell Street Bridge is constructed

1929 Great Depression begins

1937 Commencement of Buffalo Rapids Irrigation Project

1940 Establishment of Dawson County Junior College (later Dawson Community College)

1950s Glendive population increases to over 5,000 as first area oil-boom begins

1960 Glendive population peaks at more than 7,000. Population of Dawson County is 12,314

1980 Glendive population is 5,978; that of Dawson County is 11,805

1980s Second Glendive-area oil boom

1990 Glendive population is 4,802; that of Dawson County is 9,505

Suggested Reading

+⊨━━⊨+

THIS GUIDEBOOK depends heavily on William A. Babcock's "Historical Resources Survey: Glendive, Montana," prepared for the Glendive Area Chamber of Commerce and Agriculture in 1987. That report, which contains a comprehensive bibliography, and the accompanying site forms are available at the

Montana State Historic Preservation Office
1410 8th Avenue
P.O. Box 201202
Helena, MT 59620-1202
(406) 444-7715

The single most useful source for general Glendive-area historical developments is Marie MacDonald's *Glendive: The History of a Western Town* (Glendive, 1968), which provides excellent information on area ranchers and ranches in addition to the history of Glendive itself. *Our Times, Our Lives* published by the Dawson County Tree Branches (Glendive, 1989) provides good biographical sketches of Glendive-area residents and a good overview of several Glendive businesses. *The Climate, Soil and Resources of the Yellowstone Valley*, published by the Pioneer Press, (St. Paul, Minn., 1882) provides invaluable information on the layout of Glendive. The best sources for information on Glendive buildings are the early newspapers: the Glendive *Times*, 1881–87, the Glendive *Independent*, 1884–1916, and the Dawson County *Review*. Ella Schloss's "Glendive Business Locations, 1880–1976," on file at the Glendive City Library and the Frontier Gateway Museum, and Avis Anderson

69

and Eileen Melby's *Ranchers, Railroaders and Retailers of Glendive: Their Houses and Families, 1881–1930* (Wibaux, Mont., 1985) are also invaluable. The works by Schloss and Anderson and Melby are exhaustively researched studies of Glendive's commercial and residential buildings, respectively.

On the prehistory of the area, see William P. Eckerle and Stephen A. Aaberg's report, "PaleoIndian Archeological and Geological Investigations in the Blue Mountain–Glendive Area of Eastcentral Montana," prepared for Glendive Forward in 1990.

Two Glendive repositories are excellent sources of information on the history of Glendive and Dawson County: the Glendive City Library and the Frontier Gateway Museum. Useful library holdings include its Montana Collection, newspapers, and vertical files. The museum contains an excellent photograph collection, maps, and manuscripts.

Index of Building Sites